PEOPLE WHO HELP US

Popcorn

Firefighters

Honor Head

WAYLAND

Explore the world with **Popcorn -** your complete first non-fiction library.

Look out for more titles in the Popcorn range. All books have the same format of simple text and striking images. Text is carefully matched to the pictures to help readers to identify and understand key vocabulary.
www.waylandbooks.co.uk/popcorn

First published in paperback in 2012 by Wayland

Wayland
Hachette Children's Books
338 Euston Road
London NW1 3BH

Wayland Australia
Level 17/207 Kent Street
Sydney NSW 2000

Produced for Wayland by

White-Thomson Publishing Ltd
www.wtpub.co.uk
+44 (0)845 362 8240

Editor: Jean Coppendale
Designer: Clare Nicholas
Picture Researcher: Amy Sparks
Series consultant: Kate Ruttle
Book consultant: Patrick Tyler,
    Community Safety Prevention,
    Devon and Somerset Fire and Rescue Service
Design concept: Paul Cherrill

Head, Honor.
    Firefighters. -- (Popcorn. People who help us)
    1. Fire fighters--Pictorial works--Juvenile literature.
    I. Title II. Series
    363.3'78-dc22
ISBN: 978 0 7502 6839 4

First published in 2010 by Wayland
Copyright © Wayland 2010

Wayland is a division of Hachette Children's Books,
an Hachette UK company.
www.hachette.co.uk

Photographs:
Alamy: SHOUT 21/22b; Corbis: 11; Devon and Somerset Fire and Rescue Service: 8/23b; Dreamstime: Michaela Stejskalova 18; Fotolia: Monkey Business 1/10; Getty Images: Ana Mosquera 17/23t; iStock: Shaun Lowe 9/23m/cover; Photolibrary: Anton Luhr 19; Shutterstock: Four Oaks 4, Andrew Magill 13/2, EML 15/22t, Lilac Mountain 20; Wayland: Chris Fairclough 5, 16; Franklin Watts: Andy Crawford 6, Chris Fairclough 7, 12, 14.

Contents

Firefighters

Firefighters help us when there is a fire. In a fire people can be badly burnt and buildings can be damaged.

Firefighters learn how to put out fires safely before they can work as a firefighter.

Firefighters live at a fire station when they are on duty. Most fire stations have a kitchen, shower room and bedrooms.

Firefighters eat their meals in the kitchen.

Sometimes firefighters can be on duty for a whole day and night.

5

Fire engines

While the firefighters are waiting for a call to a fire, they check the equipment on the fire engines.

The fire equipment is carefully packed away in the fire engine.

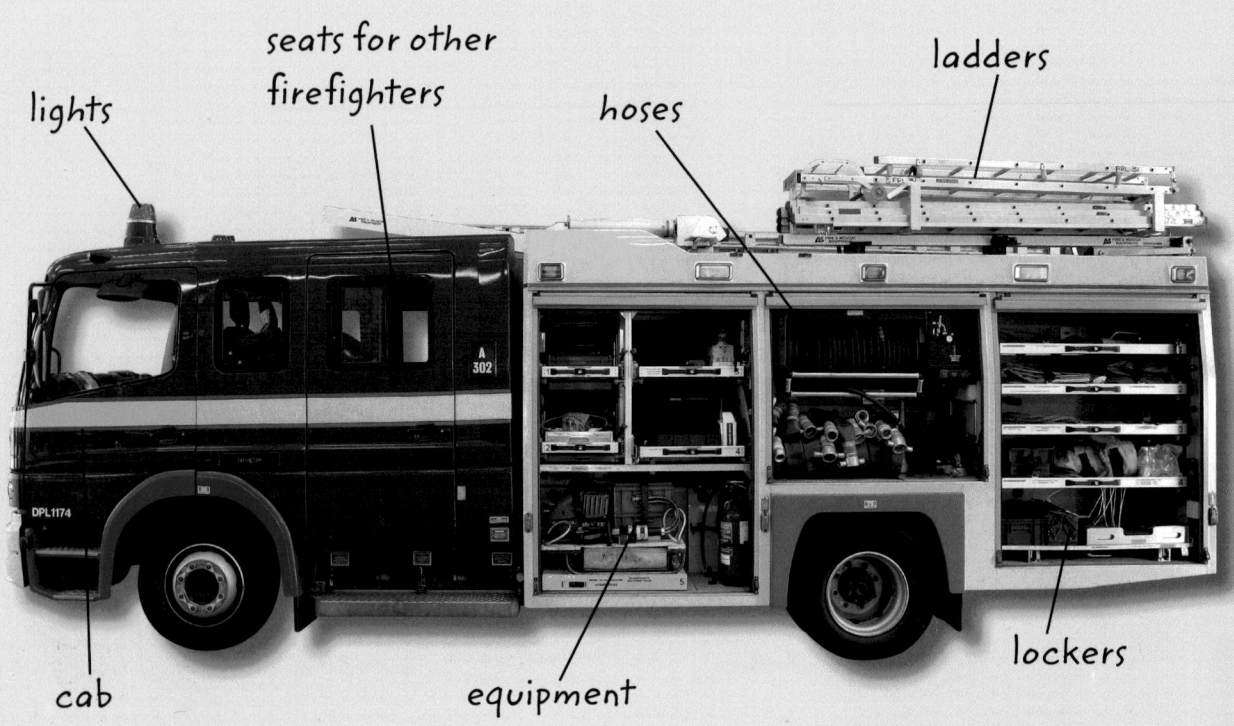

lights

seats for other firefighters

hoses

ladders

cab

equipment

lockers

When someone calls for the fire service, an alarm bell at the fire station makes a loud noise. The firefighters race to their fire engine.

The flashing blue light means that cars have to let the fire engine go first.

flashing blue light

 # Fire!

When they reach the fire, the firefighters quickly check what has to be done. They might need to use a ladder to rescue someone.

The firefighters' ladders are very long to reach the top of buildings.

Fire spreads quickly so the firefighters have to work fast. They use hoses and water to put out the fire.

Some hoses are so big and heavy they need more than one firefighter to hold them.

Firefighters wear hard helmets to keep their heads safe.

 Team work

Firefighters have to work as a team.
Sometimes they have to work together to
rescue someone from a burning building.

Why do you think firefighters
might need an axe?

axe

All the firefighters have a radio so they can call for help if they need it.

One team member checks on the others by radio to make sure they are safe.

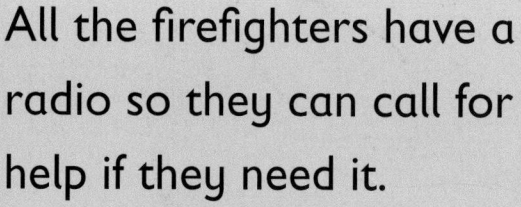

Firefighters can give first aid to people who are injured in a fire.

Fire fighting kit

Firefighters wear a special uniform to keep them safe in fires. The clothes are all fireproof so they will not catch on fire.

helmet

visor pulls down so the firefighter can see when it is very smoky

torch

stripes glow in the dark

thick gloves

Smoke from a fire can be dangerous.
If the smoke is very thick the
firefighters wear an oxygen
mask so they can breathe.

When there is a lot of smoke why is it important for firefighters to stay close together?

mask

oxygen tank

Road accident

Sometimes firefighters are called if there has been a road accident. They use special cutting tools to help rescue people who are trapped in cars.

The firefighters cut through the car to reach someone trapped inside.

If a car catches fire, the firefighters
are called to put it out before it
causes any damage.

A burning car can explode and injure people nearby.

 Calling 999

If you see smoke and you think there is a fire, leave the building straight away. Go to a nearby house or find the nearest phone and dial 999.

When you dial 999, someone will ask you which service you want. Say 'fire' or 'the fire service.'

Tell the person where the fire is.
They will give the alarm in your
nearest fire station.

The operator will ask you some questions
so he can help you as quickly as possible.

 Staying safe

Firefighters will visit you at home. They will tell you why it is important to have a smoke alarm to warn you if there is a fire.

Is there a smoke alarm in your home?

Firefighters might come to visit your school. They will tell you how to stay safe from fire and what to do if there is a fire.

What would you ask a firefighter?

21

How do firefighters help us?

Can you remember what jobs firefighters do to help us?

Match the pictures to the jobs firefighters do to keep us safe.

1. Putting out a fire.

2. Rescuing a person from a burning building.

3. Rescuing a trapped animal.

4. Putting out a car fire at a road accident.

5. Teaching you how to stop fires happening.

Glossary

canteen a public place where people eat together

duty when people are at work

fireproof clothes that do not catch on fire

first aid medical help that can be given to an injured person before an ambulance arrives

oxygen gas in the air that we need to breathe to stay alive

smoke alarm a piece of equipment you fix on the ceiling that makes a loud noise if there is smoke or a fire

uniform the work clothes all firefighters wear

Index